Hallelujah! Choco

For .....

From....

For God is great, and worth a thousand Hallelujahs. Psalm 96:4 (The Message)

Chocolate Apples

Chill an apple in the fridge, then fix it on a chopstick or toffee apple stick. Coat with melted white chocolate, turning the apple round and round to help it set evenly. If the apple is suitably cold, this shouldn't take too long. Add *Smarties* for eyes and mouth, a marshmallow for the neck and strawberry laces for mouth and neck tie. Place the apple in an empty bottle, in the door of the fridge, until it sets. Drizzle over melted dark chocolate for hair, return to the fridge and allow the hair to set.

Let's start at the very beginning

You can keep runner beans, French beans, broad beans and baked beans – they're all has-beens! Cocoa beans are my favourite! And since chocolate comes from cocoa beans, the *fruit* of the cocoa plant, I guess that makes it healthy. Maybe chocolate, being so closely related to a fruit, should count towards our 'five a day'!

My daughter, Charlotte, is very particular about food. She refuses to try courgettes, leeks, onions, kiwi, melon… the list goes on and on. However, she came to me the other day, gave me a hug and said:
> *'Mummy, I'm not really a fussy eater – after all I do like white chocolate, milk chocolate and dark chocolate, that's three different foods!'*

I won't tell her that chocolate is distantly related to a fruit or she'll demand it five times a day.

The Bible reveals that God created the cocoa plant on the third day:
> *'God spoke: "Earth, green up! Grow all varieties of seed-bearing plants, every sort of fruit-bearing tree." And there it was. Earth produced green seed-bearing plants, all varieties, and fruit-bearing trees of all sorts. God saw that it was good.'* Genesis 1:11-12 (*The Message*).

So God created the cocoa bean and as a certified Christian chocoholic I say… 'Praise the Lord for chocolate, or even Hallelujah for chocolate.'

The first people known to have discovered the secret of the cocoa bean were the ancient Maya, perhaps as long ago as

600 AD. The Maya and their ancestors harvested, fermented, roasted and ground the seeds into a paste with chilli peppers, cornmeal and other ingredients to make a frothy, spicy chocolate drink. Later the Aztecs traded with the Maya for cocoa and often required that people pay their taxes in cocoa beans – a form of Aztec money. One hundred beans would buy a slave and 10 beans a rabbit. The Aztecs also drank the cocoa in the form of a bitter chocolate drink – sugar was not available to them.

The first European who can claim to have discovered cocoa is Christopher Columbus. In 1502, he landed on an island off the coast of present-day Honduras where he was greeted by the Aztec who offered him a bag of cocoa beans in exchange for trade goods. Columbus didn't understand the importance of these beans and he hated the beverage known as *Xocolatl*. He returned to Spain without realising the economic importance of these cocoa beans. What a mistake!

During the conquest of Mexico, in 1521, the Spanish realised that cocoa was a popular drink amongst the Aztec and they shipped the beans back home.

They sweetened the drink with cinnamon and sugar and started to develop the delicious drink we know today. Almost 100 years later the rest of Europe discovered what they were missing and sweetened hot chocolate soon became the fashion.

In the mid 1600s, bakers in England started to add cocoa powder to cakes. Years later, in 1847, Joseph Fry of Fry & Sons is credited with producing and selling the world's first chocolate bar. And the rest is history…

The UK is one of the world leaders in chocolate consumption, so it's fortunate that recent research shows that chocolate, in moderation, might just be good for you! Chocolate contains flavonols, which increase good cholesterol, prevent bad cholesterol from clogging up your arteries, and make the blood less likely to clot. Dark chocolate is the healthiest type of chocolate because it contains the greatest amounts of flavonols. So… thank you, Lord, *Hallelujah! Chocolate!*

Judith Merrell, February 2009

Almond Chocolate Traybake

These marvellous fingers are quite delicious and incredibly moreish!
One just won't be enough.

Ingredients

225g (8oz) dark chocolate
2 large eggs
½ teaspoon almond essence
150g (5oz) golden caster sugar
110g (4oz) ground almonds
50g (2oz) semolina
50g (2oz) glacé cherries
50g (2oz) dried apricots

Method

1 Preheat oven to Gas Mark 4/180°C/350°F. Line a Swiss roll tin with foil.
2 Melt chocolate in a bowl over a pan of simmering water and spread over the foil, then leave to set.
3 Whisk eggs with almond essence.
4 Fold in the rest of the ingredients and spread this mixture over the set chocolate.
5 Bake in centre of oven for 20 to 25 minutes until golden in colour.
6 Cut into 18 slices and leave to cool in the tin. Once cool put in fridge to allow chocolate to set completely.

Makes 18

Choc' Chip 'n' Cherry Cookies

These scrummy cookies go down well with children – they'll probably want to help you make them too!

Ingredients

75g (3oz) soft brown sugar
125g (4½oz) soft margarine
160g (5½oz) self-raising flour
15g (½oz) cocoa powder
40g (1½oz) glacé cherries, chopped small
40g (1½oz) white chocolate chips

Method

1 Preheat oven to Gas Mark 4/180°C/350°F.
2 Cream the sugar and margarine.
3 Sift together the flour and cocoa ensuring that they are thoroughly combined, then add the cherries and chocolate chips. Fold this into the creamed mixture.
4 Form into balls (or use small ice-cream scoop) and put onto a greased baking tray, leaving room for spreading.
5 Bake for 15 minutes in the middle of the oven.

Makes approximately 18

Cocoa: 'The divine drink, which builds up resistance and fights fatigue. A cup of this precious drink permits a man to walk for a whole day without food.'
Montezuma - Aztec Emperor (c. 1466 -1520)

Choc 'n' Nut Bran Triangles

Not too rich and with the healthy addition of bran, these triangles are just right for a lunch box.

Ingredients

50g (2oz) butter or
  margarine
50g (2oz) plain chocolate
175g (6oz) soft brown sugar
50g (2oz) self-raising flour
50g (2oz) bran (broken
  All-Bran can be used)
50g (2oz) chopped walnuts
½ teaspoon vanilla essence
2 eggs, beaten

To finish

50g (2oz) plain, milk or white
  chocolate

Method

1 Preheat oven to Gas Mark 4/180°C/350°F. Grease and line a square 18cm (7in) cake tin.
2 Melt fat and chocolate in a basin over hot water, add sugar and stir until dissolved. Let this mixture cool.
3 In a separate bowl, mix together the flour, bran and walnuts. Pour the cooled chocolate mixture into this bowl.
4 Add the vanilla essence and beaten eggs and beat until smooth.
5 Pour into the tin and bake in the oven for approximately 30 minutes until the mixture is firm to the touch. Leave in tin to cool.
6 Cut into 4 equal-sized squares, then cut each square diagonally to make 16 triangles.
7 To finish, melt the chocolate in a bowl over a pan of simmering water, then dip one side of each triangle into the melted chocolate and leave until set.

Makes 16 triangles

If at first you don't succeed, stop and have some chocolate.

Chocolate Caramel Slices

These are always a firm favourite and no chocolate lover should be without this recipe.

Ingredients

Shortbread

150g (5oz) butter or
  margarine
50g (2oz) golden caster
  sugar
110g (4oz) plain flour
110g (4oz) rice flour or
  semolina

Fudge filling

110g (4oz) butter or
  margarine
110g (4oz) golden caster
  sugar
1 397g can of condensed
  milk
1½ tablespoons golden
  syrup

Topping

150g (5oz) dark chocolate

Method

Shortbread

1 Preheat oven to Gas Mark 3/170°C/325°F.
2 Line a shallow baking tray 30cm x 20cm (12in x 8in) with baking parchment.
3 Cream together the butter or margarine and sugar.
4 Sift the flours together and add to the creamed mixture.
5 Knead in bowl until smooth and press into tin making sure it is flat and even.
6 Place in centre of oven and bake for about 30 minutes until pale golden.

Fudge Filling

7 Put the butter, sugar, condensed milk and golden syrup in a heavy bottomed saucepan. Heat gently – stirring all the time.
8 When sugar is completely dissolved, bring to the boil and simmer for 5 to 7 minutes. Stir frequently and carefully to prevent mixture sticking.
9 Remove from the heat and allow to cool slightly. Pour over the prepared shortbread base and allow to cool completely.

Topping

10 Place chocolate in heatproof bowl and melt over a pan of simmering water. Pour over the cooled fudge and allow to set in a cool place. Cut into fingers.

Makes 16 fingers

Chocolate doesn't make the world go 'round', but it certainly makes the journey worthwhile!

Chocolate Heaven

We asked cake designer, Val Carroll, to devise a celebration cake for a chocoholic friend. She came up with this wonderful picture of heaven where angels are surrounded by unlimited supplies of chocolate!

Ingredients

One 23cm (9in) chocolate
    sponge split in half*

Buttercream filling

110g (4oz) butter, softened
    and mixed with

175g (6oz) sifted icing sugar

Cake covering

750g (1lb10oz) roll-out
    Belgian Chocolate cake
    covering, tinted blue

200g (7oz) (approx) flower
    paste modelling icing

200g (7oz) (approx) sugar
    paste modelling icing

Cake decorating ingredients
as underlined in method,
*(available from cake
decorating shops)*

*We used *The Big Quick Cake*
recipe from the Fairtrade
recipe book *Divine Heavenly
Chocolate Recipes with a Heart*
published by Absolute Press.
You could also use *Jane
Asher's Divine Chocolate Cake*
from the Divine Chocolate
web site at
www.divinechocolate.com

Method

1 Sandwich the two halves of the cake with filling and
    thinly coat the outside with the remainder.

2 Cover the cake in roll-out chocolate cake covering
    paste, then cut out lots of stars from the paste, paint
    with edible glue and sprinkle with edible glitter.

3 For the angels, mix together white sugar paste and
    flower paste. Leave about a quarter white to make the
    angel dresses, but colour the rest of the icing in pale
    pink, pale beige and brown for the heads, arms and
    legs. Use straw, light and dark brown, for the hair.

4 Fashion bodies in separate parts: torso, arms, legs and
    heads. Fix together with edible glue. Use a piece of
    underlined dry spaghetti as a skewer to keep the head in place.

5 Cut circles of white icing with crinkly edged pastry
    cutters. Drape over the angels like robes.

6 Squeeze the paste through a sugar craft gun to make
    hair, or fix 'a grass tube' nozzle to a piping bag. Use
    flower paste to make halos and sprinkle with glitter.

7 Cut wings from edible wafer paper, dust with
    shimmer colour and fix in place with edible glue. Mark
    angels' eyes, then place a tiny ball of white icing
    marked with a pupil in the indent. Make V-shaped
    indent for mouth and add tiny ball of icing for nose.

8 To finish, arrange white, milk and dark Fairtrade *Divine
    Chocolate* pieces around the board. Alternatively, use
    angels from a nativity set and *Milky Way Stars*.

A little too much chocolate is just about right.

Chocolate Macadamia Macaroons

Crisp and crunchy with a rich chocolate flavour, the macadamia nuts give these macaroons a unique and quite special flavour.

Ingredients

25g (1oz) macadamia nuts
25g (1oz) hazelnuts
1 egg white
85g (3½oz) golden caster
   sugar
1 level tablespoon of cocoa
   powder
Extra whole macadamia nuts,
   for decorating

Method

1 Preheat oven to Gas Mark 4/180°C/350°F and line a
   baking tray with baking parchment.
2 Blitz nuts together in a food processor or liquidizer.
3 Whisk egg white until stiff.
4 Fold in sugar, nuts and cocoa powder.
5 Drop small spoonfuls onto baking sheet – space well
   apart to allow for spreading.
6 Decorate each one with half a macadamia nut.
7 Bake in the centre of the oven for 20 to 25 minutes.
   Allow to cool on tray before cooling completely on a
   wire rack.

Makes about 10 biscuits

Seven days without chocolate makes one weak.

Chocolate Orange Cake

A splendid cake for a special celebration, why not make one and then think of a reason to celebrate!

Ingredients

Cake
110g (4oz) butter (softened)
110g (4oz) caster sugar
2 medium eggs
Zest of ½ orange
50g (2oz) plain orange
   flavoured chocolate
110g (4oz) self-raising flour

Filling and topping
50g (2oz) butter (softened)
110g (4oz) icing sugar (sifted)
Zest of ½ orange
Dessertspoon orange juice
50g (2oz) plain orange
   flavoured chocolate

Decoration
½ a chocolate orange
Orange jelly slices

Method

1 Preheat oven to Gas Mark 4/180°C/350°F. Grease and line two 17½cm (7in) sandwich tins.
2 Cream together butter and sugar until light in colour.
3 Beat in the eggs, one at a time, each time allowing mixture to become fluffy. Stir in the orange zest.
4 Blitz the chocolate for the cake in a food processor.
5 Fold the chocolate with the flour into cake mixture.
6 Divide mixture equally between the tins.
7 Bake in the centre of the oven for 20 to 25 minutes until springy to touch.
8 Cool on a wire rack.
9 For the filling and topping, cream butter with icing sugar and fold in orange zest and juice.
10 Blitz chocolate in food processor and fold into mixture.
11 When the cake is cold, sandwich together with half the buttercream icing. Spread the remaining icing on top of the cake.
12 Decorate with chocolate orange segments and orange jelly slices.

Florentines

A great treat for fruit and nut fans, best kept in the fridge until you need them.

Ingredients

50g (2oz) flaked almonds,
roughly chopped
25g (1oz) pecans,
roughly chopped
25g (1oz) chopped mixed peel
50g (2oz) glacé cherries,
roughly chopped
50g (2oz) sultanas
75g (3oz) butter
75g (3oz) light soft brown
sugar
75g (3oz) dark chocolate
75g (3oz) white chocolate

Method

1 Preheat oven to Gas Mark 4/180°C/350°F.
2 Line two baking trays with baking paper.
3 Mix together the nuts, peel, cherries and sultanas.
4 Melt the butter and sugar in a saucepan, stirring gently until the sugar has dissolved. Continue until the mixture just starts to bubble.
5 Remove pan from the heat and stir in the fruit and nuts.
6 Place teaspoonfuls of the mixture onto prepared baking trays, leaving space for spreading.
7 Bake for 8 to 10 minutes until golden brown.
8 Take the tray out of the oven and use a knife to drag in any uneven edges to make round shapes. Allow to cool a little, then ease them off the baking paper with a palate knife and place on a cooling rack until cold.
9 Melt the dark and white chocolate in separate bowls over pans of simmering water; let the chocolate cool.
10 Coat the bottom of the Florentines with the chocolate, spreading dark chocolate on half the Florentines and white chocolate on the others. NB It is important that the melted chocolate is only lukewarm when spread over the Florentines. If it's too hot the biscuits will crack.

Makes about 20

'The Spanish ladies of the New World are madly addicted to chocolate…, not content to drink it several times each day, they even have it served to them in church.'
Jean-Antheleme Brillat-Savarin (1755-1826)

Ginger Chocolate Crunch

A wonderful version of chocolate-fridge-cake that's easy to make and packs a strong punch of ginger.

Ingredients

200g (7oz) packet of ginger biscuits
200g (7oz) plain chocolate
3 tablespoons golden syrup
125g (4½oz) butter
60g (2½oz) desiccated coconut
60g (2½oz) chopped glacé or stem ginger
110g (4oz) sultanas
50g (2oz) white chocolate

Method

1 Line a 20cm (8in) square tin with baking paper. Break the ginger biscuits into small pieces into a bowl.
2 Melt together the chocolate, syrup and butter in a *Pyrex* bowl, over a pan of simmering water.
3 Remove the bowl from the pan and stir in the biscuits, coconut, ginger and sultanas.
4 Turn the mixture into the tin and roughly smooth over the top.
5 Melt the white chocolate over a pan of simmering water, then zigzag the melted chocolate over the biscuit base to make an attractive finish.
6 Chill in the fridge for two hours or more. Then, cut into 16 squares or 32 small fingers to serve. Store in the fridge.

Makes 16 squares or 32 small fingers

Any day that ends in Y is the right time to enjoy chocolate.

Hedgehog Cake

A great cake for a birthday celebration that will go down well
with the young and young-at-heart.

Ingredients

Cake

225g (8oz) margarine
225g (8oz) caster sugar
1 teaspoon vanilla essence
3 eggs, beaten
200g (7oz) self-raising flour, sifted
1 teaspoon baking powder
3 tablespoons cocoa powder
2 tablespoons milk

Icing

150g (5oz) butter
125g (4½oz) icing sugar
25g (1oz) drinking chocolate
2 dessertspoons cocoa powder dissolved in 3 dessertspoons hot water
2 tablespoons seedless raspberry jam
1 packet giant chocolate buttons
1 packet regular chocolate buttons
1 glacé cherry
2 white chocolate buttons
2 brown *Smarties*

Method

1 Preheat the oven to Gas Mark 4/180°C/350°F. Grease a large Pyrex bowl. We used a 3 litre (5¼ pint) bowl, but a 2.5 litre (4½ pint) bowl would also work.
2 Cream the margarine and sugar until light and fluffy. Add the vanilla essence. Beat in the eggs, a little at a time, with 4 or 5 spoonfuls of the flour.
3 Fold in the remaining flour along with the baking powder and cocoa. Add one or two tablespoons of milk if the mixture is too dry.
4 Turn into your Pyrex bowl and bake for about 1 hour or until the top is springy and a skewer comes out clean. Leave in the bowl to cool.

To decorate

5 Beat together the butter, icing sugar, drinking chocolate and dissolved cocoa powder until smooth and creamy.
6 Cut the cake in half horizontally and sandwich back together with 2 tablespoons of seedless raspberry jam and a couple of big spoonfuls of the butter icing.
7 Cut a thin slither of cake off two sides of the circle to make a point for the snout.
8 Cover the whole cake in butter icing and lift it onto a cake plate. Stick halved chocolate buttons into the icing to look like spines. Use large buttons in the top and smaller ones lower down.
9 Add a glacé cherry for the nose and white chocolate buttons with brown *Smarties* stuck on top as eyes.

Save the Earth! (It's the only planet with chocolate.)

23

Marbled Chocolate Loaf

A substantial loaf that's just perfect for elevenses.

Ingredients

White chocolate mix
110g (4oz) margarine
225g (8oz) self-raising flour
110g (4oz) caster sugar
25g (1oz) grated white
    chocolate
2 medium eggs, beaten
1 tablespoon milk

Dark chocolate mix
210g (7½oz) self-raising flour
15g (½oz) cocoa powder
110g (4oz) margarine
110g (4oz) soft brown sugar
2 medium eggs, beaten
1 teaspoon cocoa powder
    dissolved in 1 tablespoon
    boiling water

Icing
75g (3oz) white chocolate
25g (1oz) plain chocolate

Method

1 Preheat oven to Gas Mark 4/180°C/350°F. Grease and line a 900g (2lb) loaf tin.
2 Prepare two separate cake mixes as ingredients list, one with white chocolate and one with plain chocolate.
3 White chocolate mix: Rub margarine into flour until mix resembles breadcrumbs. Stir in sugar and grated chocolate then add eggs and milk and mix well.
4 Dark chocolate mix: Sift together flour and cocoa then rub margarine into them until mix resembles breadcrumbs. Stir in sugar then add eggs and the cocoa powder dissolved in water and mix well.
5 Place alternate tablespoons of each cake mix into the tin, alternating the colours. When the tin is full, drag a knife widthways across at intervals so that there will be a marbling effect when cooked.
6 Bake for 1 to 1¼ hours until firm.
7 To decorate, melt the white chocolate in a bowl over simmering water and spread over the top of the loaf. Once set, melt plain chocolate in same way and drizzle over the top.

A balanced diet is equal quantities of white chocolate and dark chocolate!

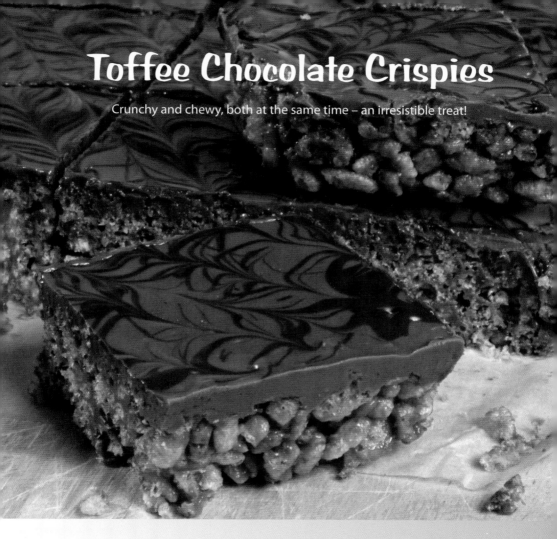

Toffee Chocolate Crispies

Crunchy and chewy, both at the same time – an irresistible treat!

Ingredients

3 *Mars* bars, finely chopped
50g (2oz) butter
125g (4½oz) rice crispies
175g (6oz) milk chocolate
25g (1oz) dark or white
    chocolate

Method

1 Line a 20cm (8in) square tin with baking paper.
2 Melt the *Mars* bars and butter in a large heatproof bowl over a pan of simmering water. Stir frequently until the mixture is well blended. You will find that it doesn't melt into a smooth liquid but stays thick and gloopy!
3 Gradually stir in the rice crispies until they are all covered in the melted chocolate-toffee mixture.
4 Tip the mixture into the tin and press down with the back of a spoon.
5 Melt the milk chocolate in a heatproof bowl over a pan of simmering water. Melt the dark or white chocolate in another bowl in the same way. Pour the milk chocolate over the top and then zig zag either plain or white chocolate over the top of this to create a two tone effect.
6 Leave in the fridge for 2 to 3 hours to set before cutting into squares.

Makes 20 pieces

Stress wouldn't be so hard to take if it were chocolate covered.

Triple Chocolate Muffins

These generous-size muffins are great for when you've missed breakfast!

Ingredients

225g (8oz) caster sugar
225g (8oz) soft margarine
3 large eggs
210g (7½oz) self-raising flour
25g (1oz) cocoa powder
    plus 1 teaspoon
75g (3oz) plain chocolate
    chopped into pieces
75g (3oz) white chocolate
    chips
1 tablespoon milk

Method

1 Preheat oven to Gas Mark 4/180°C/350°F.
2 Cream sugar and margarine together until light and fluffy.
3 Add 3 beaten eggs to this mixture.
4 In a separate bowl, sift together the flour and 25g (1oz) of the cocoa powder making sure they are well combined. Fold this into the mixture together with the chocolate pieces and chocolate chips.
5 Make a chocolate paste by blending the remaining 1 teaspoon of cocoa powder with 1 tablespoon of boiling water. Add this to the mixture, with the milk. Spoon the mixture into muffin cases and bake in a moderate oven for 25 to 30 minutes.

Makes 10-12 muffins

There's nothing wrong with me that a little chocolate won't cure.

Simply Divine

Sadly, many farmers in developing countries, who grow crops like cocoa, coffee, tea and bananas don't earn enough to pay for the things that we take for granted such as access to clean water, medicines and a child's education. All too often they don't get a fair deal for their work.

Next time you're in the supermarket look out for the FAIRTRADE mark. All of the recipes in *Hallelujah! Chocolate!* can be made with Fairtrade chocolate which is available in milk, plain, and white bars along with many other exciting flavours.

We particularly like *Divine Chocolate*, which is totally delicious and a key player in the Fairtrade movement.

Sometimes you may have to pay that little bit extra for Fairtrade products, but it's worth it to know that the farmers were paid a fair price and were given decent working conditions.

A little bit extra goes a long way, as the members of the Kuapa Kokoo Co-operative in Ghana, who produce cocoa beans for Divine Chocolate and co-own the company, can affirm.

At the moment, Kuapa farmers are only able to sell a small percentage of their cocoa beans to Fairtrade companies because there is not yet enough demand from consumers. However, more shops will stock Fairtrade products if customers demand it and demonstrate that they will buy the goods.

Gladys Okai, Kuapa Kokoo, Ghana

I am a member of the Kuapa Kokoo Co-operative in Ghana. They have done a lot for us thanks to the extra income from Fairtrade.

At first we used to fetch water from rivers but today we have a hand-dug well with a pump which was funded by the Kuapa Kokoo Farmers' Trust. In the past we walked for three miles deep into the forest to fetch water. The water was not clean and there were worms in it. We had to sieve it through a towel before drinking it. Now, thanks to Kuapa, we have a well in our village and we no longer have to walk long distances to get water. The water is clean and when we drink it we don't get sick.

Children now go to school early and farmers go to their farms earlier and we have time for other things, because we don't have to keep fetching water. Now we can fetch as many buckets as we like! Kuapa Cocoa Trust is pa pa paa – the best of the best! Before Kuapa it was a huge task getting water. May God bless Kuapa!

Photos: Kim Naylor

Chocolate Baskets

These attractive baskets are easy to make and can be filled with your own choice of fruit and whipped cream.

Ingredients

110g (4oz) dark chocolate
One fairy cake or trifle sponge
6 teaspoons sherry, sweet wine
or orange juice
120ml (4 fl oz) double cream
12-14 strawberries (approx
225g or 8oz)

Mint leaves

Method

1 Break chocolate into squares and melt in a Pyrex bowl over a saucepan of simmering water.
2 Use the melted chocolate to coat 6 paper cake cases. Tip and tilt the cases from one side to another until the insides are completely covered. Put in the fridge to set. If possible, leave overnight.
3 Once set, gently tear off the paper. Keep the chocolate baskets in the fridge while you are making the filling.
4 Slice the fairy cake or trifle sponge into six small pieces. Put a piece of cake in the base of each chocolate basket. Pour a teaspoon of sherry (or juice) over the sponge cake.
5 Whip the cream until it forms soft peaks.
6 Reserve six strawberries for decoration and finely slice the remainder.
7 Fold the chopped strawberries into the cream, then place a spoonful of this mixture into each chocolate basket.
8 Decorate each basket with a single strawberry and a sprig of mint. Return the baskets to the fridge and remove just before serving.

Makes 6 baskets

Give thanks to the Lord for he is good; his love endures for ever. ...for he satisfies the thirsty and fills the hungry with good things. **Psalm 107:1 and 9 (NIV)**

33

Chocolate Cherry Gâteau

An exotic variation on a Black Forest Gateau – just right for a dinner party dessert.

Ingredients

Cake
3 medium eggs (separated)
150g (5oz) golden caster sugar
75g (3oz) plain flour
25g (1oz) cocoa powder

Cherry filling
425g (15oz) can black cherries
    including juice
1 dessertspoon arrowroot or
    cornflour

Cream filling/coating
275–300 ml (approx ½pt)
    whipping cream
2 tablespoons cherry brandy
A little grated chocolate for
    decoration

Method

1. Preheat oven to Gas Mark 4/180°C/350°F. Line a 20cm (8in) springform tin with baking parchment.
2. Whisk together eggs and sugar until pale and thick. Sift together flour and cocoa powder and gently fold into egg mixture. Pour mixture into prepared tin and bake in centre of the oven for 25 to 30 minutes until well risen and firm to touch. Cool on a wire rack.
3. Drain cherries, reserving juice, and remove stones from all but 12 cherries (these are for decoration). Make juice up to 150 ml (¼pt) with water. Mix a little of this liquid with arrowroot or cornflour. Heat rest of liquid in a saucepan and then add to mix.
4. Return all the juice to pan and bring to the boil, continuously stirring. Cook for a minute, then remove from heat and allow to cool and add cherries.
5. Whisk cream until it holds soft peaks, then carefully whisk in cherry brandy.
6. When cake is cold, cut in three horizontally. Put the bottom layer on the serving dish and spread with cherry mixture. Put the next layer on cherry mix and spread with about a third of the cream.
7. Add the top layer and cover the whole cake with the remaining cream. Decorate with the 12 cherries and grate a little dark chocolate in the centre.
8. Chill for at least 2 hours for the flavours to develop.

Serves 12

All I really need is love, but a little chocolate now and then doesn't hurt!
Lucy in *Peanuts* by Charles M. Schulz

Chocolate Espresso Cups

These are a great way to round off a dinner party, but take them out of the fridge a little beforehand or the mousse will be too firm.
Thanks, Mark, for this stylish recipe!

Ingredients

275ml (½ pint) single cream
400g (14oz) dark chocolate
(at least 70% cocoa solids)
25g (1oz) butter
25g (1oz) icing sugar to taste
2 egg yolks, beaten
2 tablespoons of *Tia Maria*
(Use brandy, rum or
Cointreau as a variation.)

To decorate
A little double cream
8 raspberries or similar

As a variation, melt a little
white chocolate with
some cream and use this
as a topping, turning
the espresso cups into
cappuccinos.

Method

1 Simmer the cream in a heavy pan for a couple
of minutes.
2 Break up the chocolate and add it to the cream.
Remove from the heat.
3 Once the chocolate has melted and blended with
the cream, add the butter and stir in well.
4 Add the alcohol of your choice. You can add too
much, so taste as you go.
5 Taste and add sugar at this point, if needed.
6 When the mixture has cooled a little, add the egg
yolks. The mixture must be cool enough so as not to
cook the egg, but warm enough to still be pourable.
A balloon whisk is good for this.
7 Pour the chocolate into 8 small espresso cups.
8 Chill for about 30 minutes.
9 Beat double cream until thick, and pipe a rosette of
cream on each mousse. Add a raspberry to the centre
of each cream rosette. Alternatively, decorate with
grated chocolate, strawberries or similar. Best eaten
the same day.

Serves 8

Chocolate, coffee, men... some things are just better rich, dark and strong.

Chocolate Orange Crowns

This soft and creamy mousse has a wonderful hint of fresh orange. If you have time to present each mousse in an orange crown the effect will be stunning.

Ingredients

3 oranges
40ml (1½fl oz) hot water
40g (1½oz) butter
110g (4oz) marshmallows
175g (6oz) dark chocolate
200ml (7fl oz) double cream
Zest of two oranges
Juice of ½ a large orange,
  sieved

Method

1 Cut the three oranges in half using alternate slanting cuts to create 6 crowns. Scoop out the flesh with a grapefruit knife. It doesn't matter if some of the orange is left behind it all adds to the flavour. *(Put the orange segments on one side for a fruit salad or melon and orange starter.)*

2 Put the water, butter, marshmallows and chocolate in a saucepan and melt together over a low heat, stirring frequently until the mixture is smooth. Remove from the heat and leave to cool a little.

3 Whip the cream until it forms soft peaks, then add the orange zest.

4 Stir the orange juice into the chocolate mixture, then combine the two mixtures.

5 Place spoonfuls of the mixture into the orange crowns, so that the mousse forms a peak in the centre. Or, if you have time, chill in the fridge for 10 minutes and then put the mousse into a piping bag and pipe swirls into the orange crowns.

6 Allow to set in the fridge for a couple of hours. Remove a few minutes before you wish to serve as the flavour and texture are best when not too cold.

Serves 6

Chocolate Roulade

This melt in the mouth chocolate dessert with its creamy chestnut filling makes an excellent Christmas Log, but it's too good not to be enjoyed all year round!

Ingredients

Roulade
175g (6oz) dark chocolate
3 large or 4 medium eggs
   (separated)
175g (6oz) golden caster sugar
2 teaspoons instant coffee
1 tablespoon hot water

Chestnut Filling
300g (10½oz) vacuum-packed
   peeled chestnuts (available
   in tin or packet)
100ml (3½ fl oz) milk
75g (3oz) golden caster sugar
1½ tablespoons brandy or
   your favourite liqueur
150ml (¼ pt) double cream

To assemble
50g (2oz) icing sugar

Method

1 Preheat oven to Gas Mark 4/180°C/350°F. Line a large baking tray with baking parchment.
2 Break up chocolate and melt in a bowl over a pan of simmering water. Whisk egg whites until stiff. Whisk egg yolks with sugar and fold in the melted chocolate.
3 Dissolve coffee in one tablespoon of hot water and carefully fold into chocolate mix. Fold in the whisked egg white and pour into prepared tin.
4 Place in centre of oven. Bake for about 25 minutes, until firm. Remove from oven and leave to cool in the tin for a few hours with a piece of foil over the top.
5 Meanwhile make the chestnut filling: simmer chestnuts in the milk with the sugar for about 20 minutes, until chestnuts are tender.
6 Leave to cool slightly, then place all in a food processor or liquidizer with the brandy and whiz together.
7 Whip cream until it forms soft peaks. When chestnut mix is completely cold, fold in the whipped cream.
8 To assemble roulade: place foil on work surface and sprinkle with icing sugar. Tip cake onto icing sugar and remove parchment. Spread with chestnut filling, then using the foil, roll up roulade from the long edge.
9 Ease roulade onto serving tray and sift with icing sugar, then store in fridge until required.

Serves about 10

Hot Chocolate Pudding

This pudding is s-o-o good that it's quite indescribable. It works especially well with gluten-free flour.

Ingredients

210g (7½oz) butter plus extra for greasing ramekins

210g (7½oz) dark chocolate (at least 70% cocoa solids)

3 medium eggs and

3 medium egg yolks

6 tablespoons golden caster sugar

3 heaped teaspoons gluten-free flour, sieved - or use regular plain flour

Method

1 Preheat oven to Gas Mark 7/220°C/425°F.

2 Generously butter eight 175ml (6 fl oz) ramekins – place a circle of baking parchment in the base of each.

3 Break up chocolate and place with butter in a bowl over a pan of simmering water. Stir occasionally until melted and shiny.

4 Using an electric whisk, whisk together all the eggs and the sugar until light in colour, thick and frothy.

5 Whisk in the chocolate mixture until no streaks remain.

6 Fold in the flour, then equally divide mixture between ramekins.

7 Place ramekins on a baking sheet and put in the oven.

8 Bake in a hot oven for 10 minutes until the outside of the puddings are set – the centre should be runny.

9 Gently cut round each mould and turn onto a warm plate. Dust with cocoa powder if desired and serve with whipped cream or similar.

Serves 8

Profiteroles

A pyramid of profiteroles makes a delicious, decadent centrepiece for a party buffet.
They'll disappear before your eyes!

Ingredients

Choux buns
40g (1½oz) butter
   or margarine
60g (2½oz) plain flour
2 eggs, beaten

Filling
275ml (½pt) whipping cream
Raspberry jam (optional)

Sauce
110g (4oz) dark chocolate
25g (1oz) butter
2 tablespoons water, brandy
   or liqueur of your choice

Method

1 Preheat oven to Gas Mark 6/200°C/400°F. Line a baking tray with baking parchment.
2 Place the butter in 150 ml (¼ pt) water in a saucepan and bring to the boil. Meanwhile sift the flour.
3 Remove saucepan from the heat and tip flour into the water and butter mix.
4 Beat until mixture becomes smooth and leaves the sides of the saucepan.
5 Next whisk in the beaten egg, just a little at a time. After each addition, beat until the mixture is a smooth and glossy paste.
6 Place mixture into a piping bag fitted with a plain, 1cm (½ inch) nozzle.
7 Force small blobs of paste, about the size of a walnut, onto baking tray using a wet knife to detach each one. Leave space for choux buns to rise.
8 Bake in centre of the oven for 25 to 30 minutes until well risen.
9 Cut each profiterole and return to the oven for five minutes to dry out, then cool on a rack.
10 Whisk the cream until it holds soft peaks, then fill each profiterole with jam (if used) and cream. Pile in a pyramid on a serving dish.
11 Put chocolate sauce ingredients in a heatproof bowl and melt over a pan of simmering water. Pour over the pyramid of profiteroles.

Serves 8

I'd give up chocolate, but I'm no quitter.

Raspberry Chocolate Dream

Raspberries and white chocolate are just made for each other, and you can make this delicious, dreamy dessert just as sweet or fruity as you like.

Ingredients
75g (3oz) white chocolate
150ml (¼ pint) double cream
225g (8oz) Greek yoghurt
250g (9oz) raspberries

Method
1 Melt the white chocolate with 2 tablespoons of double cream in a Pyrex bowl over a pan of simmering water. Remove from the heat and allow to cool a little.
2 Whisk the remaining double cream until it forms soft peaks, then add the Greek yoghurt and whisk again.
3 Gently add and whisk in the chocolate mixture.
4 Stir in about half the raspberries, allowing some of them to break up and turn the mixture a pleasing shade of pink. Taste the mixture and if it's too sweet add a few more raspberries.
5 Put a few raspberries in the bottom of each wine glass, reserving a few for decoration. Divide the creamy mixture between 4 wine glasses. Decorate each one with a raspberry and a sprig of mint or a chocolate curl.

Serves 4

Isn't it strange that a 200g bar of chocolate can make a person gain a whole kilo in weight?

Tangy Cheesecake

The sharp citrus flavour of the cheesecake contrasts well with the dark chocolate to make a wonderful zesty dessert.

Ingredients

200g (7oz) pack ginger biscuits
50g (2oz) butter
110g (4oz) dark chocolate
2 x 250g (9oz) tubs
   mascarpone cheese
Finely grated zest & juice
   of 2 limes
Finely grated zest and juice
   of 1 small lemon
25 to 50g (1 to 2oz) sifted icing
sugar, according to taste

To make chocolate leaves

Select leaves that have a
clear vein structure. Wash
and dry thoroughly. (If the
leaves are not dried properly
a white bloom appears on
the chocolate.) Coat the back
of the leaves with melted
chocolate and leave in the
fridge to set. Grasping the
stalk, gently peel off the green
leaf to find a chocolate replica.
Rose leaves work well.

Method

1 Line the base of a 20cm (8in) round springform cake
   tin with a circle of baking paper.
2 Seal the ginger biscuits inside two plastic bags and
   crush with a rolling pin.
3 Melt the butter in a saucepan and mix in the biscuit
   crumbs. Press this mixture into the base of the tin.
4 Chop 50g (2oz) of the dark chocolate into rough chips.
5 Whisk together the mascarpone cheese, lime zest and
   juice, lemon zest and juice. Sweeten with icing sugar
   according to taste.
6 Spread over the biscuit base, scattering the chopped
   chocolate around the outside edges as you spoon
   in the mixture. This ensures that pieces of chocolate
   are visible around the edge when you turn out the
   cheesecake, while the top remains white.
7 Fork the mixture into a slight peak in the centre.
8 Leave to set in the fridge for an hour or more.
9 Decorate the top with a slice of lime and chocolate
   leaves made from the remaining chocolate.

Serves 10

Forget diamonds – chocolate is a girl's best friend!

Tipsy Chocolate Gateau

This delicious gâteau is always popular at parties! Thank you, Pam, for giving us your recipe.

Ingredients

7 eggs
200g (7oz) caster sugar
1 dessertspoon oil
150g (5oz) self-raising flour
50g (2oz) drinking chocolate
1 heaped teaspoon cocoa
powder

Filling and topping

2 teaspoons coffee powder
2 teaspoons caster sugar
1 tablespoon boiling water
150ml (¼ pint) water
3 tablespoons rum
4 tablespoons seedless
raspberry jam
400ml (14 fl oz) double
cream, whipped
50g (2oz) dark chocolate

*If you don't have large flan
tins, use two Swiss roll tins
and make a rectangular
gâteau.*

Method

1 Preheat oven to Gas Mark 7/220°C/425°F.
2 Grease and line two round 28cm (11in) loose
bottomed flan tins. Brush the greaseproof paper
lightly with oil or melted butter.
3 Whisk eggs and sugar until double in size, and texture
of softly-whipped cream. This will take 3–4 minutes; it
is important to warm bowl before you start. Drizzle in
the oil very slowly while continuing to whisk.
4 Sieve the flour, drinking chocolate and cocoa into
a bowl, then fold in very gently. Divide the mixture
between the two tins and gently level the surfaces.
5 Bake towards top of oven for 12 to 15 minutes until
the centre springs back when touched.
6 Leave to cool in the tin for 10 minutes, then remove
the baking paper and continue cooling on a wire rack.
7 Dissolve the coffee and sugar in a tablespoon of
boiling water, then add the rest of the water and rum.
Drizzle half this liquid over the base of the sponge.
Spread the base with raspberry jam and about a third
of the whipped cream. Place the second sponge on
top and drizzle the rest of the liquid over the top.
Spread with whipped cream.
8 Melt the chocolate and drizzle over the top in
concentric circles, draw a skewer through the circles
to create a feathered effect.

Serves about 20

*I have this theory that chocolate slows down the aging process.... It may not be true,
but do I dare take the chance?* **Anon**

Winter Crumble

This delicious crumble topping works well with many other fruit, but bananas are especially good with chocolate!

Ingredients

75g (3oz) margarine or butter
175g (6oz) plain flour
50g (2oz) dark soft brown sugar
75g (3oz) plain chocolate chips
50g (2oz) chopped nuts
4 or 5 large bananas
2 tablespoons milk
2 tablespoons chocolate liqueur (optional)
50g (2oz) plain chocolate, grated

Method

1 Preheat oven to Gas Mark 6/200°C/400°F.
2 Rub fat into flour until mixture resembles fine breadcrumbs.
3 Stir in the sugar, chocolate chips and nuts.
4 Grease an ovenproof dish, then slice bananas and arrange in dish.
5 Drizzle milk and liqueur and sprinkle grated chocolate over the bananas.
6 Spoon crumble mix over the bananas and press down gently.
7 Bake for 35 to 40 minutes in the centre of the oven

Serves 4 to 5

After about 20 years of marriage, I'm finally starting to scratch the surface of what women want. And I think the answer lies somewhere between conversation and chocolate.
Mel Gibson

53

Chocolate Coconut Ice Cubes

Wrap a few of these delicious sweets in cellophane as a special gift, or serve them with coffee at the end of a dinner party.

Ingredients

450g (1lb) golden granulated sugar
150ml (¼ pt) milk
150g (5oz) desiccated coconut
1 tablespoon cocoa powder – sifted
175g (6oz) plain or milk chocolate for coating

Method

1 Line a tin 20cm x 15cm x 3½cm (8in x 6in x 1½in) with baking parchment.
2 Dissolve sugar in the milk, over a low heat, without stirring.
3 Bring to boil and simmer gently for about 10 minutes.
4 If you have a jam thermometer, you want 112.5°C (240°F) 'soft ball' stage.
5 Quickly stir in the coconut and cocoa, and pour immediately into lined tin.
6 Leave in a cool place to set.
7 Before completely cold, cut into squares to produce cubes.
8 Melt chocolate in a bowl over a pan of simmering water. Using a cocktail stick to hold each cube, coat with the chocolate.
9 Place cubes on a baking tray lined with baking parchment and place in fridge to set.

Makes about 48

I'm not overweight, I'm just chocolate enhanced.

Easy Easter Truffles

These truffles are unbelievably smooth and rich and make a wonderful grown-up gift at Easter or, in fact, any time of year!

Ingredients

100ml (3½ fl oz) double cream
200g (7oz) dark chocolate
(70% cocoa solids)
2 tablespoons rum, brandy,
Cointreau or similar
A little cocoa powder for
dusting
2 ginger biscuits or 5 *Amaretti*
biscuits, in fine crumbs

Method

1 Warm the cream in a pan without letting it boil.
2 Break up the chocolate and stir into the cream until melted.
3 Add the spirit or liqueur and stir until smooth and glossy.
4 Pour into a bowl and chill in the fridge until set (at least 2 hours).
5 Cool your hands in a bowl of cold water and dry thoroughly, then dust your fingers with cocoa powder. Roll teaspoons of the mixture into small balls, then roll in cocoa powder. Alternatively, place a square of cling film over the palm of your hand and use this to roll the truffles into balls.
6 As an alternative to cocoa powder, roll half the truffles in ginger or *Amaretti* biscuit crumbs.
7 Place in paper sweet cases and store in the fridge in a plastic box.

Makes 20 sweets

I've never succumbed to love at first sight, but I love to succumb to chocolate at first sight.

Minty Chocolate Treats

These sweets are fun to make with children who always enjoy bashing up the biscuits!

Ingredients

150g (5oz) plain chocolate
25g (1oz) butter
½ teaspoon peppermint
 extract
110g (4oz) digestive biscuits,
 crushed

To coat
75g (3oz) melted chocolate,
 plain, milk or white

Method

1 Break up the chocolate and put in a pan with the
 butter and 2 tablespoons of water. Heat gently
 until melted.
2 Stir in the peppermint extract then the biscuit crumbs
 and mix thoroughly. Allow to cool.
3 Turn onto a strip of foil. Using the foil, shape into a
 cylindrical roll about 4cm (1½in) in diameter. Cut into
 about twenty 5mm (¼in) slices.
4 Dip one side of each slice into the melted chocolate
 and place chocolate side up onto greaseproof paper.
 Leave until chocolate has set. Repeat, to cover the
 other side.

Makes 20

The secret of friendship is give and take – you give me chocolate and I'll take it!

Index

Fruit Kebabs

Chop small pieces of fruit and arrange on barbecue skewers. Melt 3 or 4 squares of chocolate with one tablespoon of cream per person. Place the chocolate sauce in individual small bowls or ramekins. Guests will love to dip their kebabs into the chocolate sauce before savouring the fruit.